NEW VANGUARD • 145

BRITISH SUBMARINES OF WORLD WAR I

INNES McCARTNEY   ILLUSTRATED BY TONY BRYAN

First published in Great Britain in 2008 by Osprey Publishing,
PO Box 883, Oxford, OX1 9PL, UK
PO Box 3985, New York, NY 10185-3985, USA
Email: info@ospreypublishing.com

Osprey Publishing is part of the Osprey Group.

Transferred to digital print on demand 2014.

First published 2008
1st impression 2008

Printed and bound in Great Britain

A CIP catalogue record for this book is available from the
British Library.

ISBN: 978 1 84603 334 6

Page layout by Melissa Orrom Swan, Oxford, UK
Index by Alan Thatcher
Cartography by Peter Bull Map Studio
Typeset in Sabon and Myriad Pro
Originated by PDQ Digital Media Solutions

The Woodland Trust
Osprey Publishing are supporting the Woodland Trust, the
UK's leading woodland conservation charity, by funding the
dedication of trees.

www.ospreypublishing.com

Author's note
I would like to thank the staff at the Royal Navy Submarine
Museum for their great help over the years that I have studied
British submarine conflict. In particular, Debbie Corner, Curator of
Photos, was most helpful in identifying several not-so-well-known
images for this book.

Editor's note
For ease of comparison between types, imperial measurements
are used almost exclusively throughout this book. The following
data will help in converting the imperial measurements to metric:

1 mile = 1.6km
1lb = 0.45kg
1 yard = 0.9m
1ft = 0.3m
1in. = 2.54cm/25.4mm
1 gal = 4.5 liters
1 ton (US) = 0.9 tonnes

All images are courtesy of the Royal Navy Submarine Museum

CONTENTS

BRITISH SUBMARINES OF WORLD WAR I

INTRODUCTION

The contribution that British submarines made to the Allied war effort in 1914–18 far outstripped any expectation that would have been made of it at the outset of the war. Small in size and primarily made up of obsolete designs, the Royal Navy Submarine Service grew in strength and confidence as the war progressed, and, when given the right operating conditions, was able to yield some important successes.

In the Baltic the crucial iron ore trade between Germany and Sweden was all but curtailed by no more than five British submarines. The small Baltic flotilla also largely interrupted the activities of the German High Seas Fleet in this sector and claimed two important surface units.

The Submarine Service won four Victoria Crosses – Britain's highest award for gallantry – in the Dardanelles. In so doing it almost wiped out the Turkish Navy and halved its Merchant Marine. The contribution of so few submarines to such an achievement stands in stark contrast to the losses on land during the campaign.

In home waters British submarines were used in a largely defensive role until late in the war, when their capability as an anti-U-boat weapon brought a steady stream of successes from 1917 to 1918. Nevertheless, constant patrolling of the Bight of Heligoland brought several encounters with the High Seas Fleet, where several larger enemy warships were damaged.

Although losses were high, British submarines had shown that these small craft possessed the capability to deny large stretches of the sea to the enemy. Unlike a battleship a submarine could be replaced rapidly. Some 150 new submarines joined the fleet during the war, while 54 were lost. At the Armistice Britain's submarine force was ascendant and had been imbued with a fighting tradition it subsequently has never lost.

DESIGN AND DEVELOPMENT

Pre-war coastal classes

The earlier B- and C-Classes were employed during the war, notably in the Baltic and Dardanelles. Ostensibly obsolete, their roles had to be matched carefully to the right theatres, with their ultimate withdrawal from frontline service being inevitable.

Eleven B-Class submarines were built from 1904 to 1906. They constituted further British development of the coastal design pioneered by John Philip Holland and first adopted by the Royal Navy in 1901. The displacement was nearly double that of the A-Class (completed from 1903 to 1908), but the boats were still limited in endurance and capability. The increased reserve buoyancy over the A-Class was a distinct advantage, reducing the possibility of being swamped in poor weather. Yet the B-Class still had no internal bulkheads and few crew comforts. A major design breakthrough was the retrofitting of hydroplanes forward as well as aft, which dramatically increased underwater stability. B-Class submarines were armed with two 18-in. torpedo tubes.

During World War I B-Class submarines played a largely subsidiary role in home waters and in the Mediterranean. Only B10 was sunk during the war, when it became the first submarine ever to succumb to air attack, whilst at Venice. B11 won notable acclaim for the sinking of the Turkish ironclad *Messudieh*, in the Dardanelles, winning the Submarine Service's first Victoria Cross. Only B3 served throughout the war, as the others were mostly laid up when worn out or converted into patrol craft.

HMS/m H8 under way. This rare aerial view, taken from Airship C2, nicely displays the features of the H-Class. Note the streamlined shape and the foldaway forward hydroplanes.

"SUBMARINE B11" COMMANDER NORMAN D HOLBROOK which sank the TURKISH BATTLESHIP "MESSUDIYEH" in the DARDANELLES DEC-13-14 "WELL DONE B11"

HMS/m B11 under way in a harbour with crew members on deck. The caption relates to her remarkable exploits in the Dardanelles, where she claimed a Turkish cruiser. The photo is pre-war, with the caption added later. Note B5 surfacing in the background.

Between 1905 and 1910 38 C-Class submarines were built. They represented a further refinement of the Holland design and were a marginal improvement on the earlier B-Class. The later C-Class vessels were fitted with two sets of hydroplanes as built, which was a major design improvement, although propulsive technology was still at a primitive level. The C-Class was the final British submarine class to be fitted with petrol engines. Moreover their battery technology barely allowed the submarine to submerge for more than a few hours. Nevertheless, 34 C-Class submarines were to operate with the Royal Navy during World War I, achieving some notable successes.

C26, C27, C32, and C35 were transported by barge and train to form part of the Baltic flotilla. C32 was scuttled in 1917 and the others in 1918, when the Russian base was closed. The remaining C-Class vessels served in

HMS/m C3 under way in Portsmouth Harbour, 1907. The crew are in 'ceremonial' positions. The two crew members at the base of the conning tower are standing on the conning tower hydroplanes. The crew are all smartly dressed but are not in full uniform. This is obviously an official event as A5 and A6, which are beyond C3, are similarly engaged. The two battleships are HMS *Barfleur*, on the left, and HMS *Duncan*, alongside in the background. Packed with explosives, C3 was used to destroy the mole at Zeebrugge in 1918.

home waters in operational and training roles. Four were lost to enemy action. To their credit, these obsolete submarines sank three U-boats. C3 was used in the Zeebrugge Raid in April 1918, where it was deliberately blown up beside the mole.

The D-Class submarine

The development of the D-Class began in 1905 and marked a departure in British submarine design. For the first time, the Admiralty designers were tasked with developing a submarine that could be employed on offensive operations along an enemy's coastline. Previously British submarines had been conceived for deployment in the harbour and coastal defence role. The major technological leap forward that was required to build an overseas class of submarine was the diesel engine. It took five years of trial and error to create the right levels of reliability and performance with the diesel propulsion unit. This meant that D-Class submarine production did not get into full swing until 1910. Originally, 19 were to be built, but after eight had been completed, production was switched to the newer, larger E-Class.

To develop an overseas submarine meant that a series of revolutionary introductions had to be made. Not least was the need to increase significantly the displacement of the D-Class over previous designs. Range and surface performance meant a larger submarine was needed. The D-Class, therefore, was twice as large as any British submarine that had preceded it. The hull shape was also radically different. This was because of the introduction of external ballast tanks, a stern torpedo tube, and an "over-under" configuration for the two forward tubes. The D-Class also incorporated two diesel engines, each driving its own propeller shaft, leading to the first twin-propeller British submarine.

Moreover, the D-Class was also the first British submarine to be fitted with a deck gun, with D4 being the first so fitted. Initially, a foldaway mounting was used, but during the war it was found to be more practical to fit a permanent one.

Half of the D-Class submarines built were lost in action in World War I.

D-Class design characteristics

D1 was laid down in 1907, and D8 was completed in 1912. D1 through D6 were built at Vickers, Barrow, and D7 and D8 were built at Chatham Dockyard.

The hull marked a new direction for British submarines, with the adoption of a saddle tank design. This offered a number of advantages. With single-hull designs outside pressure affects the control structures within the pressure hull, causing a weakening of the hull's integrity. Mounting saddle tanks for the stowage of ballast external to the pressure hull allowed for a much larger reserve buoyancy, making the submarine easier to handle and safer to operate, and, therefore, less likely to founder in the event of water ingress. D-Class reserve buoyancy was designed to be 25 per cent, a great improvement over the 10 per cent seen on earlier classes, which was widely believed to have been too small to have prevented a number of diving accidents.

D-CLASS SPECIFICATIONS	
Overall length	162ft
Maximum width	20ft 6in.
Surface displacement	500 tons
Submerged displacement	620 tons
BHP engines	1,200
Surface speed	16kt
BHP motors	550
Submerged speed	9kt
Range	3,500 miles at 10kt
Fuel	Diesel, 35 tons
Submerged endurance	9 hours at 5kt
Armament	1 x 12-pdr QF gun, 3 x 18-in. torpedo tubes
Complement	25

HMS/m D4 at harbour stations, pre-war. D4 was the first British submarine to be equipped with a deck-gun. In 1918 she turned U-boat killer, sinking UB72 off Weymouth.

A key area for consideration was improved habitability for the crew on longer overseas patrols. The D-Class could offer much more internal space than previous designs because of its greater size and the saddle tank design. Crew exhaustion could therefore be obviated by better living conditions being incorporated into the larger hull.

The D-Class submarine was the first British design to be fitted with a stern torpedo tube. This was considered necessary due to the anticipated sluggish underwater manoeuvrability that caused the loss of a target as the submarine turned to line up its forward torpedoes. Another advantage was the ability to retire from action with a torpedo ready and pointing in the direction of any pursuing enemy.

In the long lists of 'firsts' for the D-Class submarine, perhaps one of the most revolutionary was the fitting of a deck gun. This greatly increased the

1. HMS/m B11

The B-Class submarine continued the evolution of the first submarines built by the Royal Navy. Construction ceased in 1906 in favour of the larger C-Class. Endurance of the B-Class was still very limited, which in reality meant that they could be used for defensive purposes only. They were armed with two 18-in. torpedo tubes. Initially, the design proved unstable while submerged, but the fitting of hydroplanes forward of the conning tower corrected this problem.

HMS/m B11 was the submarine in which the Submarine Service won its first Victoria Cross. In an audacious act that involved penetrating the Dardanelles defences, the little B11 was able to torpedo and sink the Turkish cruiser *Messudieh* while at anchor. Barely able to negotiate the treacherous currents within the straits, B11 was almost lost on a sandbank as she made her escape under a hail of Turkish shellfire.

2. HMS/m C27

The C-Class submarine was the last of the petrol-powered line of British submarines and marked the furthest refinement of the Holland design. Nevertheless, the class still suffered from the same weaknesses as its predecessors: limited range and short underwater endurance. Crew comforts were negligible, and the class suffered from the limited operational options of short patrols and harbour defence.

HMS/m C27 was completed in 1909. At the outset of the war, she was based in home waters, where, on 20 July 1915, in harness with a trawler, she torpedoed the German submarine U23. Shortly thereafter she was stripped down and sent via Murmansk to join the Baltic Flotilla. In 1918 she was scuttled to avoid capture.

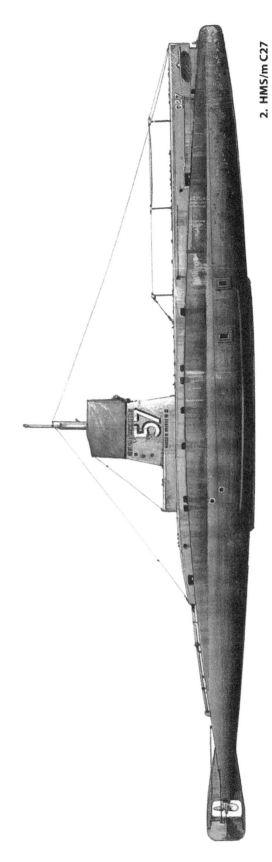

A

1. HMS/m B11

2. HMS/m C27

HMS/m D4 in dry dock. This photograph shows the unique rotating design of the D-Class bow cap. Note also the saddle tank along the starboard side. By placing the ballast outside the pressure hull, more room was available inside.

Unidentified D-Class submarine returning from patrol. The large ensign was employed as a precaution against attack by friendly forces. Sadly this measure did not prevent the tragic loss of D3 to a French airship in the Channel in 1918. Note the tiny unprotected bridge and saddle tank on the port side.

submarine's offensive power, allowing it to sink unarmed ships, finish off torpedoed targets, and fire at the shore, while saving its scarce torpedoes for worthwhile targets. Some British submarines made great use of the deck gun during World War I.

A curious feature of British submarine deck gun design was the disappearing mounting, which first made an appearance on D4. It was brought to firing position by the use of compressed air. The reason for the adoption of this cumbersome system seems to have been based on concerns over corrosion of the gun in the sea environment as much as to the submarine's streamlining. In reality, the folding gun took time to deploy in action and was widely abandoned during World War I. Other means of preventing corrosion were adopted, and, with the gun on a fixed mount, action could commence as soon as the submarine surfaced.

Propulsion by twin diesel engines was a major breakthrough in British submarine design and was the key feature in the development of the overseas submarine design. The increased hull design also allowed sufficient batteries to be carried for the submarine to remain submerged throughout the hours of daylight. This ability was critically important when operating off an enemy coast.

Vastly superior to all previous classes, the D-Class formed the basis of an entire generation of overseas submarine classes that followed. All eight submarines that were built operated exclusively in home waters during the war. Four were lost to enemy action, while D-Class submarines claimed two U-boats during World War I.

The E-Class submarine

Arguably Britain's best submarine of World War I, the E-Class was a logical progression in development from the D-Class. These boats were larger in displacement and were the first British submarines to incorporate transverse bulkheads, which divided the submarines internally into three compartments. This offered better survivability in the case of flooding.

The outbreak of World War I led to an expanded programme of submarine construction. The Emergency War Order of November 1914 called for the building of 38 E-Class submarines. As war production got going, construction times nearly halved over those built pre-war.

E-Class design characteristics

E1 was laid down in 1912, and E56 was completed in 1916. There are enough design differences to segment the E-Class into three groups: E1 through E8, E9 through E20, and E21 through E56. They were built by government and private shipyards, with two (AE1 and AE2) being supplied to Australia.

The E-Class submarines built up to 1914 were fitted with only a single forward tube, one aft tube, and two transverse tubes amidships. The transverse tube was considered necessary because of the theoretical possibility of collision with the target when firing bows on. This design feature was never proved to be of any specific use and was largely abandoned in later classes. With the Emergency War Order, an additional forward tube was specified. Hence, from E9 onward, five torpedo tubes were carried. A minimum of one spare torpedo per tube was carried internally. Spare torpedoes could also be carried externally.

Unlike the earlier versions that were built, the later E-Class submarines were designed to be fitted with a deck gun as standard. During the war, a wide combination of gun types was adopted. The most common was the 12-pounder quick-firing gun, although several other types were used. Mountings were both of the fixed variety and the folding type, first adopted by the D-Class.

The six E-Class minelayers were fitted with ten vertical mine chutes that ran through the outer ballast tanks. Each carried one mine, allowing for the sowing of a 20-mine field. To enable this technology to be fitted, weight was saved by removing the two transverse torpedo tubes. In all other regards these submarines were standard to the E-Class design and could, therefore, operate offensively with gun and torpedo. Minelaying proved dangerous work because the mines themselves were volatile and the fields tended to be sown in the

HMS/m E9 leaving Reval for the last time. Under the command of the enigmatic Max Horton DSO, this submarine had a major influence on the war in the Baltic. Note the summer camouflage pattern and the small deck gun. The bridge is protected only with a canvas screen, making for tough conditions in the bitter Russian winter.

E-CLASS SPECIFICATIONS

Overall length	E1: 176ft; E9 onward: 180ft
Maximum width	22ft
Surface displacement	E1: 652 tons; E9 onward: 622 tons
Submerged displacement	E1: 795 tons; E9 onward: 807 tons
BHP engines	1,600
Surface speed	16kt
BHP motors	840
Submerged speed	10kt
Range	3,225 miles at 10kt
Fuel	Diesel, 50 tons
Submerged endurance	14 hours at 5kt
Armament	E1: 1 x 4-in. QF gun (retro fit); 4 x 18-in. torpedo tubes
	E9: 6-pdr to 6in. guns (fitted as required), 5 x 18-in. torpedo tubes
	E21: 1 x 12-pdr QF gun; 5 x 18-in. torpedo tubes
	E24, E34, E45, E46, and E51 were fitted out as minelayers
Complement	31

swept spaces of existing minefields. Any inaccurate navigation could prove disastrous.

An experiment to use E22 to carry Zeppelin-intercepting aircraft in the North Sea was abandoned. However, aircraft carrying by submarine was to re-emerge in the 1920s when M2 was converted to carry a small plane.

Of particular note are the rapid advances that had been made in the reliability of diesel propulsion, which is clearly substantiated by the fact that the two submarines ordered by the Royal Australian Navy (AE1 and AE2) were able to travel to Australia under their own motive power, something that would have been impossible a few years earlier. The Australian submarines ran for over 30,000 miles before the engines needed replacing.

E-Class submarines were fitted with 1kW wireless installations, which were later upgraded, in some cases, to 3kW. The more powerful set could broadcast reports from the Bight. In order to house this equipment, one of the transverse torpedo tubes was removed. Certain E-Class boats were also fitted with Fessenden underwater signalling gear.

The seagoing qualities of this class marked an improvement over the D-Class. This was because the submarines were larger, had larger bridges, better freeboard, and increased reserve buoyancy. The increased size made for greater crew comfort as well. As the war progressed attempts were made to improve conditions on the bridge in rough weather. This led to the adoption of brass shrouds fitted around the conning towers.

Remarkably, the maximum diving depth of the E-Class, while specified to be around 100 feet, proved to be more than twice that in service. This proved fortuitous because deeper diving depths rapidly became necessary to avoid nets and minefields, as evidenced in the Dardanelles theatre.

During World War I the E-Class more than fulfilled the expectations of its designers. It was by far the most successful British submarine class in actions against enemy warships, which included the destruction of one battleship, three cruisers, five U-boats, and seven torpedo and gunboats. Three British commanders were to win the Victoria Cross in E-Class submarines. The E-Class submarine operated in all three major theatres of the war, and seven were sent to the Baltic.

HMS/m E11 on her triumphant return from the Dardanelles after her record-breaking first patrol there. Note the absence of a deck gun – an oversight soon rectified to devastating effect. The camouflage scheme is also an interesting feature.

HMS/m E14 under way off Kephalo. This is an excellent shot of a second-group E-Class submarine. Note the open bridge and 4-in. deck gun. The absence of camouflage painting is in contrast to photos of E11 taken during the same period.

As with the D-Class, deployment throughout the war meant that losses, as a percentage of those built, were high. Twenty-six of the 57 E-Class vessels built were lost in action during World War I.

The H-Class submarine

At the commencement of the war, Britain needed to expand its submarine force rapidly. The Admiralty took up an offer from the Bethlehem Steel Company in the United States to build a number of submarines to a design then in service with the US Navy. To avoid compromising US neutrality, the first ten submarines were to be built at the Vickers facility in Montreal, Canada, from US-manufactured parts. Another ten were to be built in the United States, with the process of bringing them under British control left undecided. The Royal Navy termed these new American-designed submarines the H-Class.

The Canadian-built submarines were constructed in record time. H1 was completed in less than five months, and all ten were ready by June 1915, not

H-CLASS SPECIFICATIONS	
Overall length	H1–H20: 150ft 3in.; H21 onward, 17ft
Maximum width	15ft 9in.
Surface displacement	H1–H20: 364 tons; H21 onward, 440 tons
Submerged displacement	H1–H20: 434 tons; H21 onward: 500 tons
BHP engines	960
Surface speed	12kt
BHP motors	640
Submerged speed	9kt
Range	1,500 miles at 10kt
Fuel	Diesel, 16 tons
Submerged endurance	8 hours at 4kt
Armament	H1–H20: 1 x 6-pdr or 12-pdr QF gun; 4 x 18-in. torpedo tubes
	H21 onward: 1 x 12-pdr (some boats), 1 x .303-in. machine gun (some boats), 4 x 21-in. torpedo tubes
Complement	22

HMS/m E14 under way on exercises off Salonica. An interesting view of this famous submarine, the enlarged gun platform and saddle tanks are shown clearly.

more than six months from being laid down. The high price paid for each boat ran to $700,000. These submarines were commissioned rapidly into the Royal Navy. Six were sent to home waters and four to the Dardanelles. In June 1915, H1, H2, H3, and H4 became the first submarines to cross the Atlantic Ocean under their own power. They were escorted by the armed merchant cruiser HMS *Calgarian* and a tanker.

The ten boats built in the United States were to have different fates, mainly because the American government held them back to protect its neutrality. Surplus to British requirements by 1917, six were transferred to Chile. When America entered the war, the remaining four were sent to Britain. Only H11 and H12 arrived before the fighting was over. So, in all, only 14 were commissioned into the Royal Navy through this US–Canada route, although two of them arrived too late to see action in the war.

From 1917 British shipyards began to build a modified version of this submarine design in the United Kingdom. Consequently another eight H-Class submarines were accepted into the Royal Navy before the war ended. The H-Class was to form a keystone of the inter-war submarine force, with more being completed into 1920. H28 became the only submarine to serve on the front line in both world wars.

H-Class design characteristics

H1 through H10 were assembled at Vickers Canada, and H11 through H20 were built at Fore River, Quincy. The modified H-Class, H21 onwards, were built in British shipyards from the opening months of 1917.

Essentially a coastal submarine, the H-Class was of a single-hull design with all its ballast, fuel, water and control systems stowed inside the pressure hull. The submarine was divided into four compartments. Hermetically sealed

batteries (to prevent deadly chlorine gas being created in the presence of seawater) and automatic valves, to prevent diving below safe depths, were also new innovations. The forward hydroplanes could be folded flat against the casing for surface running and coming alongside. H1 through H20 were equipped with American-built engines and motors. From H21 onward, these were replaced with examples manufactured by Vickers.

Although half the displacement of the E-Class, the H-boats packed quite a punch. They were fitted with four forward torpedo tubes, a first in the Royal Navy. This technically made the H-Class the most powerful coastal submarine in European waters. The torpedo doors functioned in a unique way, with the outer door having to be released forward on its central pin and then rotated to expose two tubes at a time. The bow cap was sealed on a rubber gasket. The British-built H-Class submarines were lengthened to accommodate the 21-in. torpedo tube, with its reliable and heavier torpedo.

When H1 through H4 were ordered to the Dardanelles, they were fitted with either 6-pounder or 12-pounder guns. The other H-Class submarines were fitted with an assortment of different weaponry, from machine guns (in World War II) to 12-pounders, as and when required.

The H-Class was fitted with 3kW wireless apparatus and Fessenden underwater communication equipment. The upper control space within the conning tower could be used to con the boat and also housed a second periscope.

In service the H-Class boats performed well and proved to be reliable, although initially regarded with suspicion by the British submariner. The streamlined shape allowed for a quick diving time that outstripped that of the British designs. They handled well underwater, primarily due to the placement of a rear set of hydroplanes to counteract the forward weight of the four torpedo tubes. The durability of this class, along with its superior handling qualities in shallow coastal waters, meant that it remained in service into World War II. Seven H-Class submarines operated offensively in 1940–41, and several were used in training roles up to 1945. This successful design remained in service with navies around the world well into the Cold War.

Four H-Class submarines were lost in action in World War I; three in home waters and one in the Adriatic. This reflects a low percentage compared to those deployed. However, these submarines were not active in high numbers until the war was well under way.

HMS/m H10 diving off the east coast after her refit in April 1916. H10 was lost to unknown causes in the North Sea in January 1918.

H-class submarine bow torpedo tubes. With four forward 18-in. torpedo tubes, the H-Class was among the most powerful coastal submarine classes in European waters during World War I.

HM submarines alongside. From outboard: E35, D3, H5, H8 and E54. Note the smaller dimensions of the H-Class. This is an unusual photograph as it shows E54, H8 and D3, all of which were commanded by LtCdr B. L. Johnson, Royal Navy Reserve (RNR). D3 was the first boat to be commanded by a Canadian of the Royal Canadian Navy (RCN), Lt William Maitland-Dougall. She was bombed and sunk in error by a French airship in the English Channel on 12 March 1918. H5 was also sunk by accident, being rammed by the merchant ship *Rutherglen* in the Irish Sea ten days before D3 was lost.

Later coastal classes

The ten R-Class submarines were built to carry out anti-U-boat work but came into service too late to make an impact. Nevertheless, they are worthy of note for being a design that was much ahead of the times. The role of the British submarine in the last years of the war seemed increasingly to be to target U-boats. However, successes were few, even though sightings were not uncommon. The R-Class was designed as a U-boat killer. It was given an unprecedented underwater speed of 15 knots and a bow salvo of six 18-in. torpedo tubes. One propeller shaft was powered by two electric motors. The small diesel engine for surface propulsion was hardly powerful enough to re-charge the submarine's batteries.

In service only one R-Class submarine fired at a U-boat, although it missed. The submarines were found to be tricky to handle on the surface and when submerged. Moreover, the lengthy battery charging time limited their practical use at sea. However, the class did pioneer important future concepts, such as hydrodynamic streamlining and use of passive sensors to detect enemy submarines.

The V-, W-, and F-Classes were all designed in the years running up to World War I as advanced coastal submarines. Interestingly all three designs used the double-hull concept; the outer hull being fined and containing systems not required inside the pressure hull. As the war started, emphasis on the construction of coastal submarines was given to the H-Class, rapidly built overseas, and, therefore, further construction was cancelled. In all, nine of these submarines saw limited service in home waters during the war.

B

HMS/m M1

The gargantuan HMS/m M1 was built on the hull of a never-completed K-Class submarine. Three M-Class vessels were built in this way and initially fitted out as monitor submarines, each carrying a 12-in. gun from a pre-dreadnought battleship. Although experimental in concept and hidden from the Germans during World War I, the technology was reported to have worked well. M2 was later converted into a seaplane-carrying submarine, and M3 was converted into a minelayer. This image shows M1 in her late-war camouflage scheme.

In November 1915 HMS/m M1 was accidentally rammed by the steamer *Vidar* and sank with all hands. The wreck was discovered by the author off Start Point in 1999.

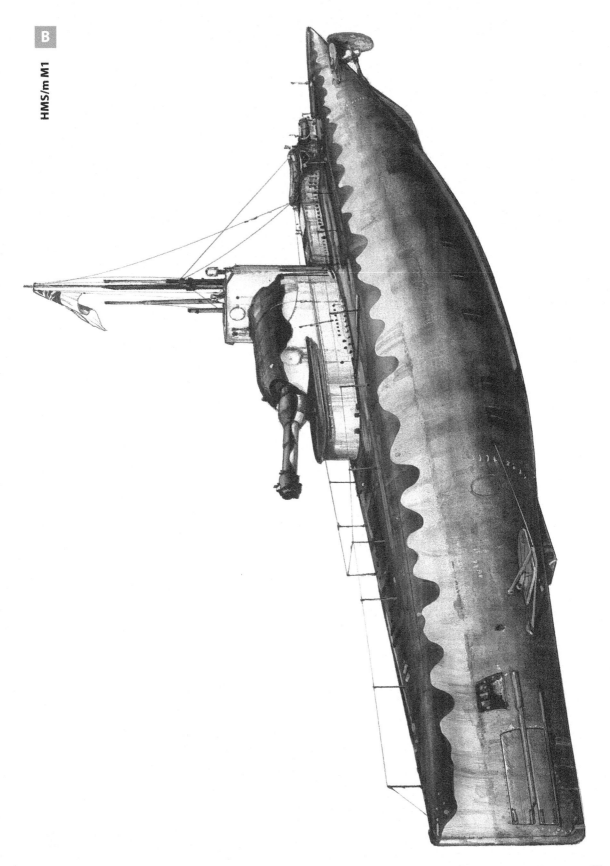

Overseas classes

The G-Class represented the Admiralty's attempt to experiment with a double-hull design for overseas submarines. In reality, it offered few advantages over the saddle tank design so successfully incorporated in the D- and E-Classes. In most other features, the G-Class submarine is closely matched to the E-Class. In all, 14 of this class were built. They all saw extensive service in home waters during the war.

The primary role of the G-Class was to patrol the North Sea, which is what it did throughout the war. In often dangerous and unrewarding patrols, the class performed adequately, accounting for two U-boats in the North Sea. Against this three G-Class vessels were sunk during the war and one shortly afterwards. Tragically, G9 was sunk by a British destroyer, which, in error, it had attempted to torpedo.

The L-Class design reverted to the saddle tank concept, since in practice it proved far simpler to construct and had few disadvantages. The L-Class represented the final evolution of the British World War I-era saddle design, going on to form the basis of the inter-war submarine fleet. A variety of armament and other new technologies was fitted to the L-Class as it evolved. Six were completed as minelayers, adopting a similar system to the E-Class.

Less than half of those built saw any service in World War I, all arriving on station late in the war. They served in home waters, where they claimed a destroyer and a U-boat in 1918. Against this, L10 was sunk shortly after claiming the German destroyer S33 off the Dutch island of Texel in the North Sea. She was the only L-Class lost in World War I.

Fleet classes

A major concern for naval planners during and after World War I was the need to develop a submarine capable of operating with the fleet. The key feature required was a high surface speed. The various fleet submarines were characterized by their uniquely large size for the time and their double-hull construction.

The J-Class was the first attempt to construct a high-speed fleet submarine. Sensibly, diesel propulsion was employed, although the resulting top speed of 19 knots was considered too slow for fleet use. Seven J-Class vessels were built, seeing action in home waters. J1 struck two German

HMS/m M1 under way at sea. This remarkable class of submarine carried a 12-in. gun from a pre-dreadnought battleship. Such firepower was unique in submarines until the nuclear age. Note the dazzle camouflage pattern and the circular foldaway gun mounting on the aft deck.

dreadnoughts with one four-torpedo salvo in November 1916. Only J6 was lost during the war, sadly, to a British vessel.

The K-Class that followed utilized steam power for surface running, which gave the speed required but doomed the class to innumerable operational problems. Besides a dozen hatches, the hulls were perforated with apertures for valves and controls. They were simply too complicated and too dangerous to use with any modern degree of safety. Nevertheless, the Admiralty placed 17 of these monsters with the Grand Fleet during World War I.

Aside from the issues arising from the use of boilers within a pressure hull, no doctrine for fleet operations existed. Not surprisingly, therefore, accidents occurred. All three of the K-Class losses during the war involved collision with friendly forces during fleet manoeuvres, fuelling the debate as to whether such submarines were anything more than a liability. No successes by K-Class submarines are recorded.

The three M-Class submarines were built upon the last three K-Class hulls already laid down. Remarkably, they were equipped with one 12-in. gun each, on top of the usual armament of gun and torpedo. The reasoning was simple: torpedoes were inaccurate and had short ranges. A submarine appearing from the depths and firing heavy shells at almost any target could be devastating. However, only M1 was completed during the war and was curiously hidden away in North Africa. It has been suggested that this

HMS/m L12 was a late arrival into action, but it wasted no time claiming a victim. On 16 October 1918 she sank the German submarine UB90 in the Skaw, one of the last U-boat kills of the war.

K-Class submarines alongside. HMS/m K14 (inboard), K22 (outboard) and K12 (centre). These huge fleet submarines were a major engineering achievement. However, tactical doctrine and the sheer practicalities of operating submarines within a high-speed fleet environment doomed the K-Class to become a tragic footnote in the evolution of British submarine design.

was because the concept was such a good one that the Admiralty did not want the enemy to copy it. Consequently, the system was never tested in anger and achieved no successes.

THEATRES OF OPERATION

The Baltic

The British fleet could not operate safely in the Baltic. The narrow, shallow seas were mined, and there were no nearby bases. Moreover, the German fleet could escape into the North Sea via the Kiel Canal. However, this area was ideal for submarine operations. An opportunity existed to send submarines into the Baltic area to interfere with German High Seas Fleet exercises and to interdict the iron ore trade with Sweden.

Consequently, in October 1914, the Admiralty sent three submarines to the Baltic: E1 under the command of LtCdr Noel Laurence, E9 under the command of LtCdr Max Horton and E11 under the command of LtCdr Martin Nasmith. The passage into the Baltic via the Skagerrak and Kattegat

HMS/m D4

The D-Class represented the first 'overseas' class of submarine built by the Royal Navy. For the first time, submarines could be used to patrol off an enemy's coastline in an offensive role. The breakthrough technology that allowed this to happen was the diesel engine. One of the key design features of British overseas submarines of this period was the saddle tank. By placing the ballast externally, much more space was available inside for the crew – a necessity on longer patrols.

HMS/m D4 was the first British submarine to be equipped with a deck gun. Torpedoes were expensive, inaccurate, and unreliable. The gun was a cheap, easy way of disposing of non-threatening targets and became the mainstay of British submarine operations throughout both world wars.

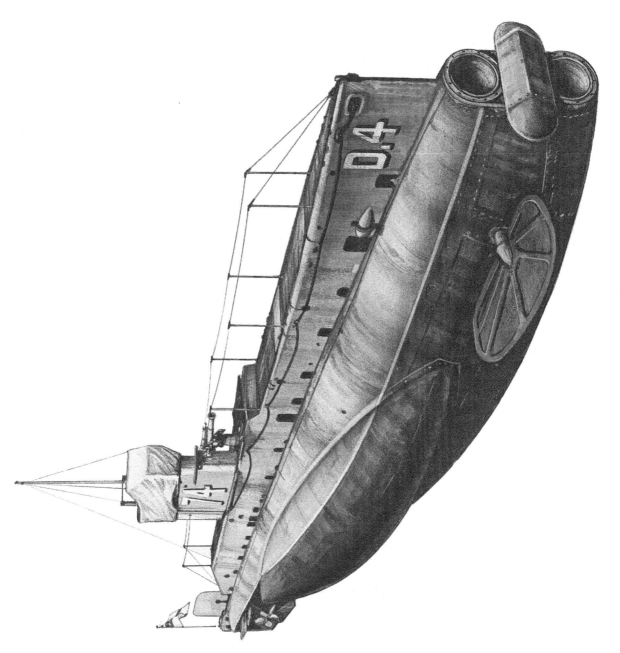

Straits and the narrow, shallow sound between Denmark and Sweden, was hazardous in the extreme. Both Horton and Laurence were able to dodge the enemy patrol vessels and make it into the Baltic. Nasmith, in E11, was not so fortunate. Having left later than the first two submarines, he found the sound well patrolled and too dangerous to attempt an entry. After avoiding being rammed and bombed, Nasmith reluctantly gave up the attempt to break through. Before he could make another attempt, he was ordered to the Dardanelles.

These three commanders were the best in the British Submarine Service, and all of them were to become household names during the war. Horton, an irreverent chain-smoking gambler with a steely manner, had already made his mark as a commander by sinking the German cruiser *Hela* in the opening weeks of the war. He would later go on to command the Western Approaches in World War II and play a critical part in the defeat of the U-boats.

The two remaining submarines to make it into the Baltic encountered much shipping and local naval forces. Laurence was unlucky to miss the cruiser *Victoria Luise*, which saw the torpedoes racing toward her just in time. This announced to the Germans that British submarines were in the Baltic. It was decided to keep them there and base them at the Russian naval base at Lapvik, where they underwent repairs.

Remarkably, in January 1915, Horton set to sea, supported by an icebreaker. The conditions were so cold that it wasn't certain that E9 would function. Horton discovered that the submarine worked fine when submerged, although her upper works froze when surfaced, needing the attention of a stoker with a chisel to keep ice from fouling the conning tower hatch. Horton made for the sound and unluckily missed a German destroyer when the torpedo veered off course and struck the seabed under its target, causing consternation in the German command, however, and curtailing operations in the area.

As the weather improved, Horton and Laurence became thorns in the side of the Germans. Operating both in harness and independently, they set about dismantling the iron ore trade and sank a number of transports, ore ships and a minelayer. In May Horton took on an escorted convoy and sank a transport under the nose of a German cruiser, forcing the convoy to double back to base. In June Horton attacked another escorted convoy and sank a transport and heavily damaged a destroyer, with only torpedo failure preventing him from adding a cruiser to his list of successes. In July Horton was again in action. This time he seriously damaged the cruiser *Prinz Adalbert*. This was a remarkable feat, due, in part, to the still, glassy sea, making any use of the periscope most dangerous. The Germans now began to refer to the Baltic as 'Horton's Sea'. Moreover, the Russian tsar decorated Horton with the Order of St George.

HMS/m E9 alongside at Reval, February 1915. Close-up of iced-up bridge with four crew members. Annotated and signed as follows: 'All good luck and with so many thanks "Scottie". Max K. Horton. 4/4/19'. The arctic conditions are well illustrated in this picture. Horton made the surprising discovery that E9 worked perfectly while submerged in winter. Only the icing up of the bridge was problematic when running on the surface.

The following month, after suffering technical problems, Laurence took to sea and damaged the battle cruiser *Moltke* in the Gulf of Riga. This was the only main element of the High Seas Fleet torpedoed during British submarine operations in the Baltic. It, in no small part, contributed to the cancellation of the German landings around Riga. The tsar sent for Laurence and awarded him the Order of St George, proclaiming Laurence 'Saviour of Riga'. The Germans came to value these two submarines as highly as a Russian armoured cruiser each, praise indeed!

The Admiralty also noted these successes, and, in the summer of 1915, bolstered the Baltic flotilla. Four of the older C-Class submarines were stripped down and towed to Archangel, Russia. From there they were barged by canal and river to Petrograd, where they were reassembled and deployed to the flotilla. They were not fully ready for service until the spring of 1916.

In the meantime another four E-Class submarines made the hazardous transit into the Baltic, risking detection and certain destruction in the deadly waters between Denmark and Sweden. E13 ran aground in this treacherous sound. Technically in neutral Danish waters, German hostility forced her scuttling with the death of half her crew. E8, under the command of LtCdr Francis Goodhart, E18 under the command of LtCdr C. Hanlahan, and E19 under the command of LtCdr F. Cromie were luckier, passing safely, though perilously, through the sound and joining up with the growing British flotilla. During her passage E8 was nearly lost and arrived in base with only a single propeller, having grounded on the seabed through the narrows while attempting to avoid the swarm of patrol vessels in the area.

These new submarines soon got into the action. German naval operations in the Baltic were continuing to support the advance of the German Army.

Without a doubt, the E-Class submarine was the finest and most successful British submarine of World War I. It was the culmination of a process of design intended to create a balanced overseas submarine, and it marked a significant improvement over the D-Class. One of the interesting features of the E-Class is its transverse torpedo tubes housed in the control room. This enabled the submarine to fire at a target when side-on. Three captains of E-Class submarines won the Victoria Cross.

HMS/m E9 will always be associated with its famous commander, Max Horton, DSO**. In E9, Horton sunk the cruiser *Hela* in 1914, the first warship sunk by a Royal Navy submarine. Horton went on with E9 to operate in the Baltic, where his attacks on German shipping were so successful that the Germans termed the Baltic 'Horton's Sea'. E9 was scuttled in the Baltic in 1918 to avoid capture.

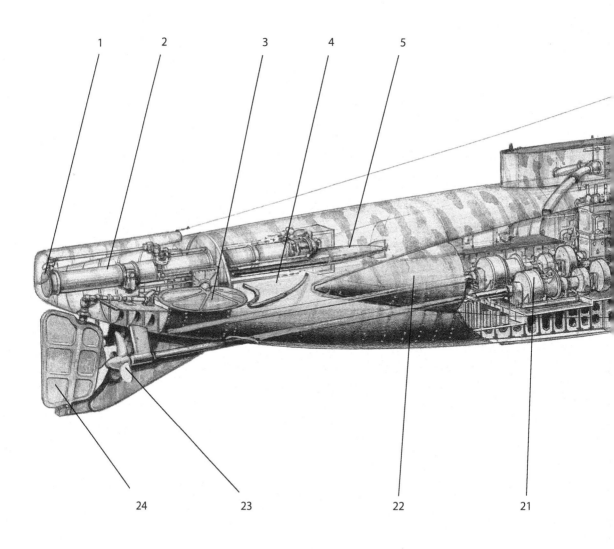

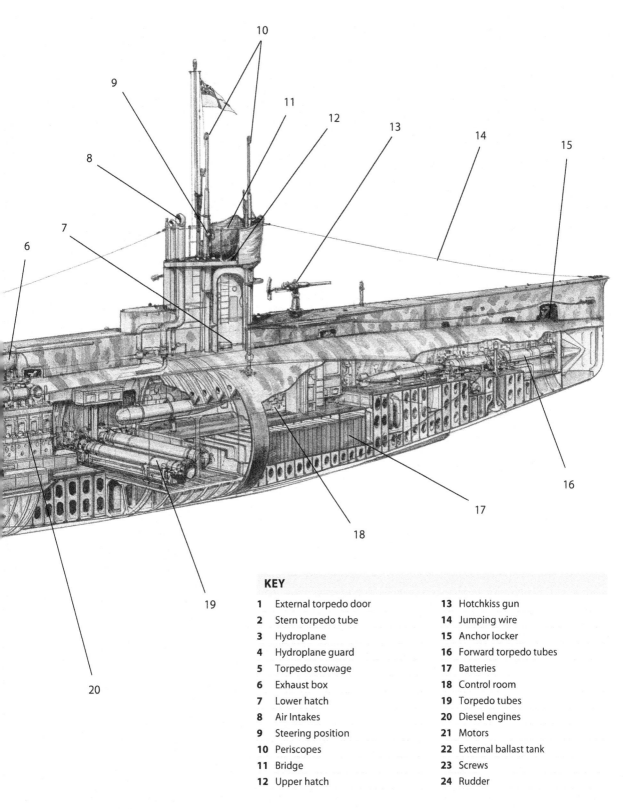

KEY

1 External torpedo door	**13** Hotchkiss gun
2 Stern torpedo tube	**14** Jumping wire
3 Hydroplane	**15** Anchor locker
4 Hydroplane guard	**16** Forward torpedo tubes
5 Torpedo stowage	**17** Batteries
6 Exhaust box	**18** Control room
7 Lower hatch	**19** Torpedo tubes
8 Air Intakes	**20** Diesel engines
9 Steering position	**21** Motors
10 Periscopes	**22** External ballast tank
11 Bridge	**23** Screws
12 Upper hatch	**24** Rudder

In October, Goodhart took E8 to sea to operate off Libau, sinking a transport on the way. Off Libau he was rewarded with the sighting of a German naval convoy. Making a textbook approach at maximum submerged speed and with judicious use of the periscope, Goodhart closed to 1,000 yards before firing his forward-facing torpedo tube. The torpedo was launched, and 60 seconds later it struck its target, igniting the magazine and blowing it to pieces. The unlucky victim of this attack was the cruiser *Prinz Adalbert*, which Horton had damaged a few months before and which had just been made fit to resume service. E8 had only a single bow tube, and it was with some luck that one torpedo made a critical hit.

LtCdr Noel Laurence (right) remains one of Britain's greatest submariners. Along with Horton, he was awarded the Cross of St George by the tsar of Russia for being the scourge of the Baltic. Later in the war Laurence became the only British submarine captain ever to have torpedoed two battleships with one salvo.

Nevertheless, this was a startling blow to the Germans, marking the first significant naval unit to have been sunk in the Baltic.

A month later, E19 was operating in the Western Baltic when she came across a German naval convoy approaching head on. Cromie took the submarine down and manoeuvred to attack. He fired the starboard-side torpedo from 1,100 yards and hit the light cruiser *Undine*. Avoiding the attentions of the attendant destroyer, Cromie finished the cruiser off with a stern shot that ignited the magazine, sending white-hot pieces of the target hundreds of yards in all directions.

The loss of these important surface units led the Germans to restrict the movement of the fleet in the Baltic for the rest of the campaign. Therefore the British submarines were mainly limited to the continuance of the interdiction of the iron ore trade with Sweden. It was this economic war, carried out largely to the letter of the law, which was to have the most significant consequences on the German war effort.

A day's work by E19 during this period serves to illustrate the impact the British submarines were having. Cromie began by intercepting the *Walter Leonhardt*, which was bound from Lulea to Hamburg carrying iron ore. The crew were taken off and put aboard another Swedish vessel, and the ship was sunk by explosive charges. Within two hours, E19 chased the *Germania* ashore after it failed to stop. She was carrying iron ore and bound for Stettin. Unable to pull her off the rocks, Cromie destroyed her where she rested. One hour later a chase began with the *Gutrune*, again laden with iron ore. After two hours she was overhauled. The crew were embarked on another Swedish ship, and the *Gutrune* was unceremoniously sent to the bottom.

Next to be intercepted was the *Nyland*. Upon inspection of her papers, it was found she was bound for Rotterdam, and she was allowed to proceed with her journey. A few minutes passed before E19 ran down the *Direktor Rippenhagen*, carrying iron ore. The German crew were, on this occasion, made temporary guests in E19 while the ship was sunk using guncotton. As soon as a suitable vessel was found, the Germans were disembarked and found themselves taking a trip to Newcastle on a Swedish freighter.

Next to be stopped was the large *Nicodemia*, which initially ran for neutral Swedish waters until two shots across the bows brought her soberly to a standstill. Her papers showed she was in transit from Lulea to Hamburg with a cargo of iron ore. The crew were put in the boats and the 7,000-ton ship blown up. The lifeboats were then towed by E19 to the safety of coastal waters.

The night passed, and, in the morning, E19 stopped the *Nike*. She turned out to be a Swedish vessel attempting to run the submarine blockade to Germany carrying iron ore. To Cromie, this made her a legitimate prize of war, and a three-man prize crew was embarked to take her into Reval. In reality, this action was contrary to international law because to be legitimate, a blockade has to be carried out night and day all year round. Clearly five British submarines could not do this. Therefore the *Nike* was later returned, cargo intact, by the Russians to Sweden. Nevertheless, in a day, Cromie had destroyed over 22,000 tons of enemy shipping. This is a remarkable score for any submarine in any theatre in either of the two world wars.

The months leading to winter 1915 marked the hiatus of British submarine successes in the Baltic. Besides sinking valuable shipping, the submarines had caused paralysis in the movement of trade in the region. Increasingly, the enemy had to expend a great amount of effort developing and operating a convoy network across the Baltic. No less than 70 torpedo boats and armed trawlers were deployed to do this. This was a drain on the limited number of smaller warships available for service with the High Seas Fleet and led to innumerable delays in the smooth transport of supplies across the Baltic Sea. In reality five submarines had virtually brought the iron ore trade to a standstill. Such a remarkable success by so small a naval force is unique in the annals of naval history.

In January 1916 Horton and Laurence were ordered to return to Britain and they reluctantly packed their bags, leaving Cromie as commander of the flotilla. Cromie's charismatic leadership was soon to be put to the test as the Russian Navy, which had steadfastly supported the British up to this point, began to fail under the dual strains of the war and the internal struggle against Bolshevism.

With the four C-Class submarines, C26, C27, C32 and C35, now ready for operations, the flotilla began to operate to a routine, which had not been possible with so few boats available previously. The C-Class submarines, being of limited duration, took up the role of coastal defence and operated primarily along the waters between Libau and Danzig. The E-Class submarines carried on as before, offensively patrolling the convoy lanes to cut off the iron ore traffic. By now targets were getting more difficult to find. The German convoy system was denuding the sea of targets, and the success of earlier times was not to be forthcoming.

Nevertheless, there was one notable success when the little C27 sank a transport in the Gulf of Riga. In May, E18 located the German destroyer V100 and scored a hit in the bows. Remarkably, the ship was saved, with the forward bulkhead holding, whilst she was towed to base by the stern. This is the last known action by E18, which perished shortly thereafter, presumably in one of the myriad minefields Germany had been laying.

When the thaw of 1917 began, British submarines again took to sea to find targets, only to find the seas deserted. No successes were forthcoming, with only C27 having the chance to attack the enemy navy and being unsuccessful.

The only other British loss in the Baltic came in October when C32 had to be scuttled in the Gulf of Riga. The submarine was suffering from a malfunctioning compass that made submerged navigation impossible. Moreover, such was the operational state of the Russian Navy at the time: C32 was not furnished with up-to-date minefield locations, nor was she in possession of the Russian radio codes. Scuttling was the only option when the submarine unsurprisingly ran aground on a mud bank.

With the Russian Revolution imminent, British submarine operations became much more difficult to maintain. Primarily, this was because of the breakdown of the chain of supplies from Britain and the increasingly fraught relationships with their Russian hosts. In one instance a British foraging party attempting to find supplies shipped by rail found a spare propeller under a hedge. Presumably the packing crate was more valuable to the looters, who had simply dumped its contents.

HMS/m E9 under way at sea in the Baltic. The 6-pounder Hotchkiss deck gun was fitted in Russia. Note the foldout platform for the gun crew. The gun was of great use during stop-and-search patrols against the iron ore trade between Sweden and Germany.

In May 1917, the flotilla moved to Hango, where it was to remain until Russia capitulated in November. Under the Treaty of Brest-Litovsk, the British submarines were to be surrendered to Germany. This was unthinkable, so consequently, with the help of a friendly Russian icebreaker, the seven remaining British submarines made for open water and were scuttled. All the crews returned to Britain except Cromie, who remained and was promoted to Naval Attaché, Petrograd. It was there that he was later killed, defending the embassy from a mob.

The Dardanelles

The waters of the Dardanelles were another area that was suited to submarine operations. Again, although small in numbers in this theatre, the presence of submarines had a hugely disproportionate impact on their enemies, scoring a remarkable, if hard-won, run of successes. For the Allies the problem with operating in the Sea of Marmora was its entrance at the Mediterranean end. Here, the currents, density layers, enemy minefields, torpedoes, searchlights, guns and uncharted shoals were a major challenge.

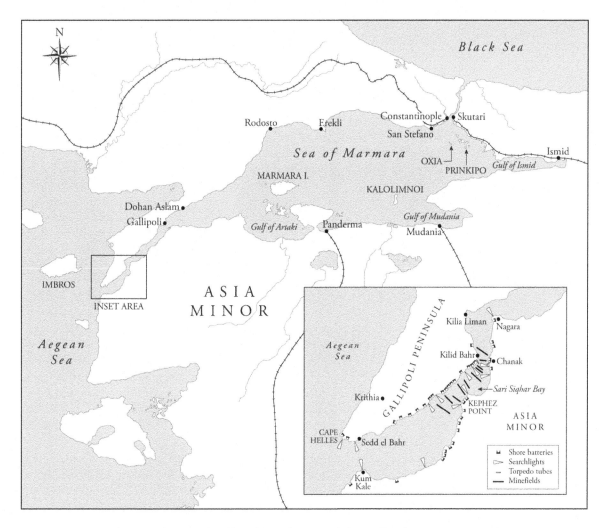

Any penetration through the Dardanelles, the narrows and the Gallipoli Strait was, therefore, fraught with difficulty and hazardous in the extreme – more so, perhaps, than the notorious sound between Denmark and Sweden.

It was the presence of two major German warships, *Breslau* and *Goeben*, at Constantinople, that naturally drew the attention of the Allies to the Dardanelles. Months before the disastrous land campaign, a naval force was built up around the island of Mudros, ostensibly to bottle up the two warships now flying the crescent flag of the Turkish sultan's navy.

The submarine contingent of the Mudros force was six Allied submarines, three of which were of the obsolete British B-Class. Powered by petrol engines and of extremely limited endurance, there was no possibility of these submarines breaking through into the Sea of Marmora. Yet the possibility did exist for a demonstration in the Dardanelles itself.

At this early juncture in the war, the primary defence in the Dardanelles was five rows of moored mines. The submarines were modified using steel tubes to protect the hydroplanes and other protuberances that could snag a mine cable. Of the three French and three British submarines present, it was B11 under the command of LtCdr Norman Holbrook that was selected for the first mission into the Dardanelles. B11 had recently had new batteries fitted, and Holbrook had some experience chasing gunboats in Turkish waters.

At 0415hrs on 13 December 1914, the little B11 made for the entrance to Turkish waters and dived. The constant current running out of the Dardanelles made progress painfully slow. After half an hour the submarine was forced to surface to remove one of the hydroplane guards that had become bent. Returning to 80 feet for another five hours brought the submarine clear of the minefields and into what Holbrook believed to be Sari Siglar Bay.

In a remarkable stroke of luck, B11 had come to periscope depth only a mile away from a Turkish warship. Holbrook had to use full power to turn the submarine to starboard and close on the anchored and unsuspecting cruiser. At a range of 800 yards, still fighting the current, Holbrook fired one torpedo aimed by eye (as was customary in World War I) and turned away. Shortly thereafter the thump of an explosion indicated that the torpedo had found its billet. A cursory glance through the periscope revealed the cruiser *Messudieh* settling by the stern with all guns firing at Holbrook's periscope. Turning away back down the straits, B11 began to make her escape. Holbrook was able briefly to witness the cruiser capsize as the shore batteries continued to rain shells around B11.

Now submerged and heading down the straits, Lt Winn, B11's First Officer, reported the compass fogged. Holbrook now had to navigate by instinct. Moreover, the current had pushed the little submarine westward across the straits into an area littered with hazardous shoals. Minutes later B11 ran onto a sandbank. Only running at full speed prevented her from grounding. As the minutes ran by B11 bounced from shoal to shoal attempting to head to safety. The light streaming in from the little portholes in the conning tower showed that it was exposed above the surface. This was confirmed by another deluge of splashes from Turkish shells. Holbrook conned the submarine by looking out of the portholes and slowly managed to bring B11 into open water and the safety of depth and thence out of the straits. Upon surfacing, the batteries were finished and the air so foul in the boat that it took all of half an hour for enough oxygen to penetrate the casing to allow the petrol engines to be started.

Holbrook returned to a hero's welcome in Mudros and within days was the toast of Britain and headline news in every newspaper. He was awarded the Victoria Cross (Winn received the Distinguished Service Order, the DSO), the first awarded to a submariner. Feted around the world (a town in Australia was renamed in his honour), Holbrook was to survive World War I, being mentioned in dispatches in 1917.

With pressure building in the Dardanelles and the possibility existing for deeper penetrations beyond the narrows, seven E-Class submarines were ordered to Mudros, six from Britain and the AE2 from Australia. The first to make the attempt was E15. However, she succumbed to the treacherous currents off Kephez and was stranded. A considerable effort was expended by the Allies to ensure she was destroyed before the enemy could make use of her. The French had already lost *Saphir* in the narrows and were to lose three more vessels before the end of the campaign. Consequently, when AE2 became the first submarine to break into the Sea of Marmora, the effort expended started to become worthwhile.

The next to make the attempt, a day later, was LtCdr Courtney Boyle in command of E14. A submerged run took E14 clear of the first minefield. Eerily, the crew heard the sound of mine cables scraping along the sides of the hull. As E14 approached the

LtCdr N. D. Holbrook, VC, the first British submariner to be awarded the Victoria Cross. The B-Class submarine was considered obsolete in 1914, and its short endurance limited its opportunities for offensive operations. In Holbrook's hands, however, it proved to be a killer of warships.

HMS/m B11's proud crew poses on deck after the attack on the Turkish battleship *Messudieh*. The submarine came close to being sunk whilst making its exit from the Dardanelles. Experience, determination and luck saw the crew survive one of the most remarkable submarine attacks in history. LtCdr N. D. Holbrook VC is seen third from left, back row. Lt Sidney Winn is fourth from left, back.

narrows, the current accelerated, and Boyle surfaced and ran awash on his diesels over the minefield at high speed, shells splashing around him. At Chanak he was forced to dive by a patrol. Boyle then torpedoed one of his tormentors and was consequently forced to remain submerged for several hours as he escaped the hunt for him, slowly entering the Sea of Marmora, motors overheating, batteries flat.

After torpedoing a transport, E14 rendezvoused with AE2 and learned that she was having a run of bad luck. This culminated with the Australian submarine being sunk the following day by a torpedo boat, leaving Boyle alone in the Marmora. Over the next few days he sank a minelayer and, with his last torpedo, a troopship, which took 6,000 Turks and an artillery battery to the bottom. With no deck gun, E14 continued the patrol with rifles, the only offensive option. Still Boyle managed to chase a transport onto the rocks and stop and search several small vessels. Ordered to return, E14 had a fairly uneventful return passage and was safely back in Mudros by 18 May. For being the first to return safely from the Sea of Marmora, Boyle was promoted to commander and awarded the Victoria Cross. He had proven that Marmora was ripe for submarine operations. Those that followed were to paralyze the Turkish supply effort to the Dardanelles front.

Martin Nasmith, in command of E11, set sail for the Sea of Marmora on 19 May. The reader will recall that Nasmith had been forced to call off his attempt to enter the Baltic a few months before. This time he was not to be so deterred. Days earlier Nasmith had flown over the Dardanelles in a biplane and noted as much as he could of all of the features, to aid navigation. So meticulous were his preparations that nothing had been left to chance. Consequently, Nasmith took a new path into the Dardanelles and found a reverse current that actually aided E11's progress toward the narrows. Aside from the usual barrage of shells, coming when the periscope was raised to get a navigational fix, and the nerve-racking scrapes of mine cables, the progress into the Sea of Marmora was a smooth one. E11 waited on the bottom until nightfall, when it was safe to recharge.

LtCdr E. C. Boyle, VC. Boyle won the second Victoria Cross for the Submarine Service for an audacious breakthrough into the Sea of Marmora in E14. The resultant patrol claimed several vessels, including a troopship, which took 6,000 Turks and an artillery battery to the bottom of the sea.

Nasmith and his officers wrote a very detailed report of their patrol over the next three weeks. It is well worth relating in some detail. The day's patrol yielded no targets, and, by late afternoon, E11 surfaced to recharge and allow the crew to bathe. In enemy waters such relaxation was welcome, if unusual, but it accorded with Nasmith's belief that a refreshed crew was an effective one. A quiet night was interspersed by another bathing session before E11 went to work. The first ship searched was a two-masted dhow that yielded nothing sinister. The terrified master refused one shilling's payment for four chickens. For the rest of the day, E11, awash, made fast to the dhow, using its mast as a lookout, as the sailing ship screened the submarine from prying eyes along the coast. In the evening, the dhow was cut loose. The following day Nasmith decided to enter Constantinople.

In the early hours of 23 May, E11 nosed its way toward the harbour approaches. At 0550hrs, a gunboat was spotted and, by 0630hrs, a torpedo had struck it amidships. The brave crew replied with its 6-pounder aimed at E11's periscope and quite remarkably hit the periscope, putting a round right through the mast and rendering it inoperative for the rest of the patrol. Shortly thereafter the *Peleng-I Derya* slid into the depths stern first. The damage to the periscope necessitated repairs, so E11 hauled off to quieter waters. By 1030hrs the scope was undergoing repairs, and the crew underwent Sunday inspection, Swedish exercise, more bathing and prayers. It was after the service that Nasmith discovered the present left by his officers of a box of cigars and some beer. He had vowed while in the North Sea not to drink until he had sunk an enemy warship.

E ### HMS/m E11 GUN ACTION IN THE SEA OF MARMORA

After E11's famous first patrol in the Sea of Marmora, where the enterprising Martin Nasmith had to recycle torpedoes that missed their targets because he had no other weapons, the need for a deck gun became obvious. During her refit at Malta, a 12-pounder was fitted to the foredeck of E11. This was the favoured deck gun for British submarines during World War I, although it wasn't always available.

In Nasmith's hands the deck gun proved a formidable weapon. It was used to finish off torpedoed ships, including a 5,000-ton troopship, and it also sank several smaller targets. Additionally, it saw much use harrying both troop movements and the new railway that supplied Turkish forces at the front.

THE HOTCHKISS 6-POUNDER DECK GUN

The 6-pounder quick-firing (QF) gun was fitted to many British submarines as an emergency measure in 1915–16. The shortage of higher calibres, especially the favoured 12-pounders, meant that initially most British submarines went to war equipped without a deck gun. However, early in the war it became obvious that a gun would be useful, and the Hotchkiss filled this role. Among those submarines so fitted were the famous E9 and E14.

Quick-firing guns used a sliding bloc that took a 'fixed' round made up of the brass case and the projectile. Fixed rounds were well suited to submarine work because they resisted damp. Moreover, the quick rate of fire was highly desirable, considering the vulnerable nature of a surfaced submarine, with an unprotected gun crew.

The following morning, the small steamer *Nagara* was sighted and brought to a stop. This elicited panic among the crew, which made for the boats. At this point an American reporter emerged from the ship and informed Nasmith that the ship's cargo was harmless and he made quickly for the boats. Upon boarding *Nagara*, however, a cargo of artillery and ammunition was found. The ship was unceremoniously blown up, and E11 was left to pursue another approaching steamer it spotted. This ship raced for Rodasto pier and hastily made fast. Nasmith approached submerged, and the torpedo that followed destroyed the ship and most of the pier as well. Clearly the target had been carrying ammunition. Now a third ship appeared. This was a paddle steamer loaded with barbed wire. It ran for shore under hot rifle fire from the bridge of E11. Once it had beached, Nasmith, determined to blow it up, approached to board. Now one hundred Turkish cavalrymen arrived on the beach to beat the submarine back with carbine fire. Nasmith took a bullet through his cap before E11 could submerge. The torpedo that followed missed the small target, and E11 withdrew.

The following morning, Nasmith returned to his earlier plan of entering Constantinople. He rounded the Golden Horn submerged, took a photograph of the harbour through the periscope, sighted a target and fired two torpedoes. One ran erratically and circled around the harbour, and the other struck the SS *Istambul*, which later foundered when beached. E11 was unable to witness this as the treacherous currents in the harbour swept the submarine onto a shallow bank before Nasmith was, luckily, able to bump her out of the shallows and back to the relative safety of the Sea of Marmora. Bathing and battery charging followed.

The next day was spent making repairs and moving the spare torpedoes into their tubes. With only five shots left, E11 was running short of torpedoes. It was therefore decided to set the torpedoes to float at the end of their runs, instead of sinking. The hope was that that they could be retrieved in the event

HMS/m E11's crew taken on 8 June 1915, after the triumphant first patrol, which won Martin Nasmith the Victoria Cross. Note the neat shell hole through the forward periscope, courtesy of a sinking Turkish gunboat outside Constantinople Harbour. Nasmith is in the centre on the bridge.

of a miss and be reused. The day's bathing was interrupted by the surprise approach of a Turkish seaplane, whose bombs fell short as E11 dived.

At 0130hrs on 27 May, lookouts spotted a battleship. A rapid, night-time surface attack was brought to an abrupt end at the point of firing when one of the escort ships turned to ram, forcing E11 into the depths, as the escort roared overhead. The following day Nasmith had better luck when a small convoy was spotted. One torpedo was fired at the largest steamer, SS *Bandirma*, which blew up and sank in less than a minute. The destroyer escort was easily evaded. At midday, a torpedo was fired at a steamship but missed. The torpedo was found floating, disarmed by a swimmer and hauled aboard, before being reloaded through the forward loading hatch. Upon investigation, Nasmith discovered the torpedo had hit but failed to detonate. In the future, recovered torpedoes were to be pushed straight into the stern tube, allowing for a rapid dive if discovered.

Lt M. E. Nasmith, VC. One of the world's greatest submariners, Martin Nasmith was a legend in the Submarine Service during World War I. His exploits in the Sea of Marmora read like a *Boy's Own* storybook. During a penetration of Constantinople Harbour, he took the time to snap a photograph through the lens of the periscope as a souvenir a first in the history of submarines.

Things remained quiet until 31 May when the SS *Madeleine Rickmers* was torpedoed off Panderma whilst embarking troops. Two days later a radio message reported that ships were again leaving Constantinople. E11 steered to intercept. At 0940hrs, the first torpedo fired struck the SS *Tecielli*, which immediately sank. Two further torpedoes were expended during the day. One was recovered and brought inboard via the new method. It was overhauled, rearmed, carried on a trolley through the submarine, and then loaded into a forward tube.

Marmora was becoming a quiet sea as shipping dried up in the presence of E11. Only the occasional destroyer

ABOVE

HMS/m E14 with gun crew in action. The 4-in. gun was a devastating weapon against shipping, shore batteries, troop columns and railways. Interestingly, in this photo, E14 displays camouflage painting.

ABOVE RIGHT

HMS/m E11 under way in harbour, at harbour stations in Mudros, 1916. During her refit in Malta she was equipped with a 12-pounder deck gun, seen here. Note the wavy lines of the camouflage scheme.

or small sailing boat came into view over the next few days. Moreover, E11 was starting to suffer from defects, so on 7 June Nasmith headed for the Gallipoli Straits and the dangerous run home. With just one torpedo remaining, he was determined to find another target. After six hours running submerged, a large troopship was spotted off Moussa Bank. The last torpedo found its mark in the SS *Ceyhan*, which rolled over to port and sank.

One last terrifying ordeal lay ahead. Off Kilid Bahr, E11 listed sharply and responded sluggishly to the rudder. Nasmith looked through the periscope and saw that a mine was snagged around the port hydroplane and was waving perilously close to the hull of the submarine, only momentum preventing certain destruction. To slow down or to surface meant death. The mine was dragged for several hours as the Dardanelles minefield was negotiated, accompanied by the usual scraping sounds. Once in open water Nasmith let on to the crew that they were carrying an unwanted passenger. By running hard astern, the errant mine was shaken loose and, finally, E11 could make for Mudros. Thus ended one of the most remarkable submarine patrols in history. Nasmith was awarded the Victoria Cross and promoted commander.

When Courtney Boyle left Mudros to take Nasmith's place, E14 had been fitted with a deck gun. This enabled the torpedoes to be saved for larger targets and still gave the submarine a decent punch to be delivered to the many dhows supplying the Turkish forces in the Dardanelles. Later, E2, E12 and E7 made successful patrols in the Marmora, also gun equipped. As the war in the Turkish sea developed, the deck gun became increasingly important. As shipping dried up, the submarines found their guns could be employed to break up troop columns, interdict the new supply railway and take on shore batteries.

In August Nasmith returned from refit and briefly joined up with Boyle in the Sea of Marmora. E11's luck continued on this patrol, whose highlights included the sinking of the Turkish battleship *Hairredin Barbarossa*, one gunboat, seven steamers, 23 sailing vessels and the railway line at Ismid, blown-up by Lt D'Oyly Hughes.

The Turks had not been idle in their attempts to stop these incursions into their inland sea. Nasmith had a brush with a Q-ship on his second patrol, which could have ended in disaster. Moreover, the minefields and nets were becoming stronger, deeper and better managed. To make matters even worse, aircraft, and even a U-boat, had also been spotted. It was the combination

SS *Bosphorus* about to sink after being attacked by HMS/m E11. Taken in the Sea of Marmora, *Bosphorus* was destroyed by fire from E11's new deck gun.

of a U-boat officer and the net barrage that was to lead to the sinking of Nasmith's replacement, LtCdr Cochrane, in E7. Enmeshed in the nets, a mine was lowered from a dinghy by Klt. Von Hiemburg of UB15, forcing the submarine to surface and surrender.

Weeks later Hiemburg torpedoed E20 in the Sea of Marmora. This event occurred as a direct result of the capture of the French submarine *Turquoise*. She had run aground on 30 October, and the commander had failed to destroy his confidential papers. A chart recovered by the enemy revealed the rendezvous position with E20. Hiemburg located the submarine, stationary on the surface, in the rendezvous position at the right time – a sitting duck.

In November Nasmith made his last patrol in the Marmora, in harness with E2. Pickings were much thinner than previously as the Turks were running supplies overland. Although several vessels were sunk and the hunting UB15 avoided, the halcyon days were a fading memory. By January 1916 the Marmora reverted to the peaceful sea of thousands of years previously.

Submarine operations continued in the Western Mediterranean for the rest of the war. These were mostly fruitless and aimed, in part, at keeping an eye on the *Goeben* and *Breslau*. In January 1918 the famous E14, now under the command of LtCdr G. S. White, was sent to Chanak to attack *Goeben*, which had been mined attempting a breakout in which *Breslau* had sunk.

E14 entered the straits on the night of 27 January. The defences were now far too strong, and yet White was able to struggle up to Chanak, where he

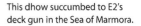

This dhow succumbed to E2's deck gun in the Sea of Marmora.

found *Goeben* had gone. E14 was put on a reverse course to run the defences one last time. On sighting a Turkish vessel a torpedo was fired, bringing the full might of the modernized defences down upon the hapless submarine. Patrol vessels raced to the scene, and depth charges began to fall through the water column. Forced to the surface, White led the crew out through the forward hatch and was killed instantly alongside 29 of his fellow crew. His posthumous Victoria Cross was a fitting epitaph to His Majesty's Submarine Service's contribution to the Dardanelles campaign.

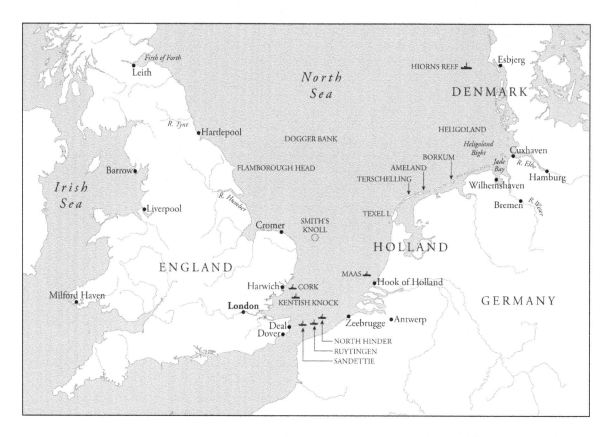

The extent to which the British submarines had contributed to the Dardanelles campaign is evident from the sinkings they achieved. They had played a very significant part in the weakening of Turkey. By 1916 the Turkish Navy had almost ceased to exist, and its Merchant Marine had been nearly halved in size. British submarines had been commanded by highly skilled officers and crewed in the same way. Showing great determination in the face of the Dardanelles barrage, they had burst through and shattered Turkish morale.

Remarkably, all this had been achieved with full regard to the safety of non-combatants and in full recognition of international law.

Home waters

This theatre of operations was not only the largest in geographical area but also utilized by far the largest number of submarines. Yet it was to prove the least successful and by far the least glamorous. Nevertheless, successes, when they did come, were notable. The majority of British submarines deployed in World War I operated from bases on the British mainland. Their roles were threefold: offensive and defensive patrolling, operations with the Grand Fleet, and anti-U-boat work.

Flotilla defence and offensive patrols

The vast bulk of the work carried out by British submarines in the home theatre was in the defence of the bases along the coast of the North Sea and on brief forays along the coastline of the enemy. Pre-war doctrine had called for most of the destroyers to be devoted to work with the Grand Fleet, leaving the defence of naval bases to the submarine force. Consequently, the earlier classes of submarine were mostly employed in this role. A-, B-, and C-Class submarines specialized in this task, in some cases right up to the last day of the war. The more modern D- and E-Class submarines, latterly supplemented with more modern designs, took up the role of offensive patrolling along the enemy's lengthy North Sea coastline.

The first success came in the early morning of 13 September 1914, and was, perhaps unsurprisingly, scored by the redoubtable Max Horton. A warship had been sighted by periscope, and E9 closed in. The following is taken from Horton's own log:

7.28am	Position 600 yards abeam of cruiser (two funnels). Fired both bow torpedoes at her starboard side at intervals of 15 seconds.
7.29am	Heard single loud explosion. Depth 70 feet, course parallel to cruiser.
7.32am	To periscope depth, observed cruiser appeared to have stopped and to have list to starboard. Dived to 70 feet.
8.35am	To periscope depth, sighted trawlers where cruiser had been. Dived 70 feet.

LtCdr G. S. White, VC. E14's last commander, White earned his posthumous Victoria Cross for bravely attempting to escape being enmeshed in the Dardanelles anti-submarine defences in 1918. He was shot and killed leading his men to safety from the forward hatch under a hail of Turkish gunfire.

The vessel he had sunk was the German light cruiser *Hela*, the first warship to be sunk by a British submarine. Two weeks later E9 added the German destroyer S116 to her tally. This led to Horton being decorated with the DSO, to which he later added two bars. Taking on destroyers was a dangerous undertaking due to their speed, size and shallow draft. His selection for the Baltic operations was undoubtedly in no small part down to these successes. They were the sum total achieved by British submarines in 1914. They came at a cost of three submarines lost.

From 1915 to 1916, the number of submarines available steadily rose, and bases at Harwich, Yarmouth, and Blyth were expanded. Successes were few as the role of submarines was mostly limited to being available to intercept raids by the High Seas Fleet. Offensive patrolling in the Bight of Heligoland and along the Norwegian coast was limited. Consequently, opportunities to engage the German Navy were few. Only E6 had opportunities to torpedo warships. She attacked and missed the battle cruiser *Moltke* in May and the light cruiser *Rostock* in October.

HMS/m K4 aground on Walney Island, 1917. The accident-prone K-boats were a liability as much as an asset. The next accident K4 was involved in killed her entire crew, when she was sliced in half by K6 during the infamous 'battle of May Island'.

39

HMS/m H5 returns to Great Yarmouth flying her Jolly Roger after sinking German U51 in July 1916. Lt John Byron RNR is on the bridge. The Jolly Roger became part of British submarine culture and was an ironic comment on the view held by the Admiralty establishment that submariners should be hanged as pirates.

Following the battle of Jutland, the number of overseas submarines available for use in home waters had reached 38. This meant a permanent watch could now be kept on the enemy coast. Patrolling in the North Sea settled into a routine, with a constant presence being kept on the Jutland Bank, at Horns Reef, and in the Bight and its entrances. Additional patrolling occurred in the Skagerrak and along the Maas. The extent of the enemy minefields in these areas was now generally understood, which made for opportunities to mine the enemy's swept channels using the new E-Class minelayers.

As 1916 came to a close, the constant presence of submarines in the eastern North Sea yielded a number of encounters with major elements of the High Seas Fleet. The most notable of these occurred on 5 November when J1, under the command of one of the heroes of the Baltic, Noel Laurence, sighted four battleships off Horns Reef. In a very heavy swell with the submarine pitching violently at periscope depth, Laurence was able to fire a spread of four torpedoes at these rare and hugely valuable targets. Under the circumstances it is remarkable that two torpedoes struck home. One hit the *Grosser Kurfurst* and the other hit the *Kronprinz*, putting both out of action for several weeks. These battleships had been used to assist in the rescue of two U-boats, and, in being damaged on a trivial operation, brought such excursions to a permanent end, earning Admiral Reinhardt Scheer a sharp rebuke from the German kaiser, Wilhelm II. Laurence remains the only British submariner to have hit two major warships with one spread of torpedoes.

The High Seas Fleet was already carrying out repairs to the battleship *Westfalen*, torpedoed by E23, and the cruiser *Munchen*, torpedoed by E38. These results were tempered by the loss of eight British submarines in the North Sea during 1916.

The rest of the war saw the emphasis shift to defeating the U-boats. Nevertheless, the dangerous and arduous routine of offensive patrolling was kept up. With the High Seas Fleet now largely inactive, encounters were few. In March 1918 E44 missed some larger warships. In April, J6 spotted German units but misidentified them as British (having been informed of the latter's presence in the area). Finally they were spotted returning, and E42 was able to damage the battle cruiser *Moltke* with a torpedo. This paltry success had come at the loss of ten British submarines.

HMS/m H5

The first ten H-Class submarines were built under a special deal by Vickers in Canada. They were of an American design, and their construction was shrouded in secrecy. The H-Class was of a simple, single-hull design, which proved to be robust and reliable in service. H-Class submarines remained in service with the Royal Navy through World War II.

HMS/m H5 served from 1915 to 1918 with the 8th Submarine Flotilla, based at Harwich and Yarmouth. In July 1916 she torpedoed the German submarine U51 off the Ems. In March 1918 H5 was misidentified as a U-boat by the steamer *Rutherglen* and was rammed and sunk with all hands. The steamer's crew were not told of their error and were awarded a bounty for sinking a U-boat, as it was deemed necessary to encourage steamships to ram U-boats.

Lt R. D. Sandford, VC, commander of C3 during its historic destruction of the Zeebrugge mole.

The mole at Zeebrugge, showing the gap blown by C3, The remains of which can be seen scattered around the breach.

The Grand Fleet

British submarines played no part in the battle of Jutland. The three submarines well situated to intercept the returning High Seas Fleet were ordered to stay on the bottom and wait for an operation that didn't take place. Clearly more use could be made of submarines.

Consequently, when Scheer again ventured out of harbour to bombard Sunderland in August, 26 British submarines were deployed to interrupt his plans. Three were already off the Ems, and two were sent to the Bight. Six submarines were placed within naval artillery range of Lowestoft, Yarmouth and Harwich. The balance of the submarines were split into three patrol groups, each headed by a destroyer and placed off the Tyne, off Harwich and off the Flanders Bight. The only damage inflicted upon the High Seas Fleet was E23's attack on *Westfalen*, mentioned earlier. Even in this case E23 had already been in its station before the British got wind of Scheer's plans.

What the Admiralty considered to be truly required was a submarine that could operate with the British Grand Fleet. This requirement led to the development of the K-Class submarine, with its unusually high surface speed. In this regard the Admiralty's plans for fleet operations with submarines were far more ambitious then those of Germany, which persisted with placing patrol lines ahead of its fleet.

No diesel-powered submarine could hope to keep up with the fleet. Even the J-Class, which was specifically designed to give a surface speed of 19 knots, was too slow. So the Admiralty designers turned to the steam turbine. The resultant K-boats were three times larger than any former British submarine and packed eight times the horsepower. Seventeen of these colossal submarines were ultimately built.

They were formed into two flotillas in 1917 and became an integral part of the Grand Fleet. In operation, they were to form a part of the forward protective screen and to submerge when the enemy fleet was spotted and to attempt to get behind it. No opportunity came to test them out in this role.

In practice the K-Class was not a success. The five-minute delay in submerging was problematic, and they did not handle well submerged. The low silhouette of a submarine could easily be missed at night, and this was a contributing factor to the disaster of the 'battle of May Island' in January 1918. K4 and K17 were rammed and sunk by accident on night manoeuvres. Three other K-Class submarines and a light cruiser were very heavily damaged, and over one hundred lives were lost. It had become clear that the

submarines, while fast, were not manoeuvrable enough to pick their way rapidly through fast-moving squadrons of ships. The short range of visibility from the conning tower made things even worse. Neither was the navigational equipment up to a standard that worked accurately alongside the fleet. The K-Class may have been a remarkable engineering achievement, but to its crews it became known as 'K for killer'.

Of the five Victoria Crosses won by the submarine arm in World War I, none is more unusual than that of Lt R. D. Sandford and C3. The Zeebrugge Raid of 23 April 1918 was aimed at blocking off Zeebrugge to the U-boats. One part of the plan featured the use of the obsolete C3, which was to be packed with explosives and rammed into the viaduct that linked the Zeebrugge mole with the mainland. C3 was able to ram the viaduct largely unhindered, but a great fire poured down on the crew as they made their escape in a small skiff carried on deck. Of the six who took part, three were badly wounded by gunfire, including Sandford. When C3 exploded, the viaduct was destroyed. Sandford took three months to recover from his wounds, only to die of typhoid shortly thereafter.

The anti-U-boat campaign

British submarines had always been on the lookout for enemy submarines in the years running up to 1917. In fact, some interesting tactics had been tried. The most enterprising was the towing of a submerged C-Class submarine by an armed trawler. In the event of a U-boat appearing, the tow could be slipped and the unsuspecting U-boat torpedoed by the hidden submarine. On 23 June 1915, this plan came to fruition when the trawler *Taranaki* was engaged by a U-boat off Blythe. Below, submarine C24 was informed, and a struggle to disengage the tow cable ensued. This achieved, C24 rudely interrupted U40's shelling of the hapless-looking trawler by placing a torpedo amidships. The ploy was again successful in July when *Princess Louise* in harness with C27 sank U23 off the entrance to the Fair Isle Channel.

Successful as these incidents may have been, the hard reality was that in the first three years of World War I, British submarines accounted for only five U-boats sunk. Now in 1917, the U-boats had unleashed a furious assault

HMS/m C27 under way. Note the original bridge with canvas screen rigged. C27 had an active war. She sank U23 in July 1915 in the North Sea, and later in the year was one of the C-Class submarines shipped to Russia to join the Baltic flotilla.

on Britain's Merchant Marine in its last episode of unrestricted submarine warfare. A major shift in emphasis in submarine deployment came with the appointment of Admiral David Beatty to the command of the Grand Fleet. He insisted on more anti-U-boat patrols and far fewer submarines being held back for defensive purposes.

Priority within existing patrol areas was now to be the sinking of U-boats. Moreover, eight C-Class submarines were allocated to keep an anti-U-boat billet off Zeebrugge, to catch the UC-type minelayers operating from their base there. A continuous patrol line was also formed, right across the North Sea from the Long Forties to the Skagerrak.

In late 1917 submarine bases were opened up in Queenstown and Lough Swilly in Ireland. The submarines based there were used to interdict U-boats operating in the Western and North-western Approaches. The Tees flotilla was also moved to Scapa Flow to cover the routes around the north of Scotland.

In 1918 submarines were also allocated to operate against U-boats in the English Channel. Notable successes in this sector were D4's destruction of UB72 and C15's sinking of UC65. In the prior case, intelligence information had led the Admiralty to station D4 mid-Channel and wait for a submarine. UB72 had been posted there to intercept the liner *Olympic*. Instead, D4 sent UB72 to the bottom with a single torpedo.

The increased emphasis on anti-U-boat work paid off with 13 U-boats being sunk by British submarines from 1917 to 1918. Six were sunk off their bases, eight in the trade routes, and four in transit. The total of U-boats sunk in the entire war was 18. This represented 10 per cent of Germany's submarine losses during the war and, while small, was a larger contribution than that achieved by the other new weapons of war: aircraft and Q-ships.

British submarine losses in World War I

Fates of the D-Class submarines
D5   03.11.14   Mined off Yarmouth
D2   25.11.14   Sunk by enemy action off Borkum
D3   12.03.18   Sunk by accident by French airship in English Channel
D6   28.06.18   Torpedoed by UB73 off Ireland

Fates of the E-Class submarines
AE1   19.09.14   Loss unknown – New Britain
E3   18.10.14   Torpedoed by U27 off Borkum
E10   18.01.15   Mined in Heliogoland Bight
E15   17.04.15   Stranded in the Dardanelles
AE2   30.04.15   Scuttled in the Sea of Marmora
E13   18.08.15   Stranded off Denmark
E7   04.09.15   Sunk by enemy action in the Sea of Marmora

HMS/m L12

A late arrival in World War I, the L-Class was the final Admiralty design to use the saddle tank concept. It was an improvement over the E-Class, offering better crew comforts and incorporating better armament. It was also capable of longer patrols. The L-Class submarine was to become one of the mainstays of the interwar submarine fleet.

HMS/m L12 was completed in June 1918 and was operational swiftly. In October she sank the German submarine *UB90* in the Skaw. Interestingly, L12 was sent into the Baltic during the War of Intervention with Russia, 1918–20. Her active service career ended in 1932 when she was scrapped.

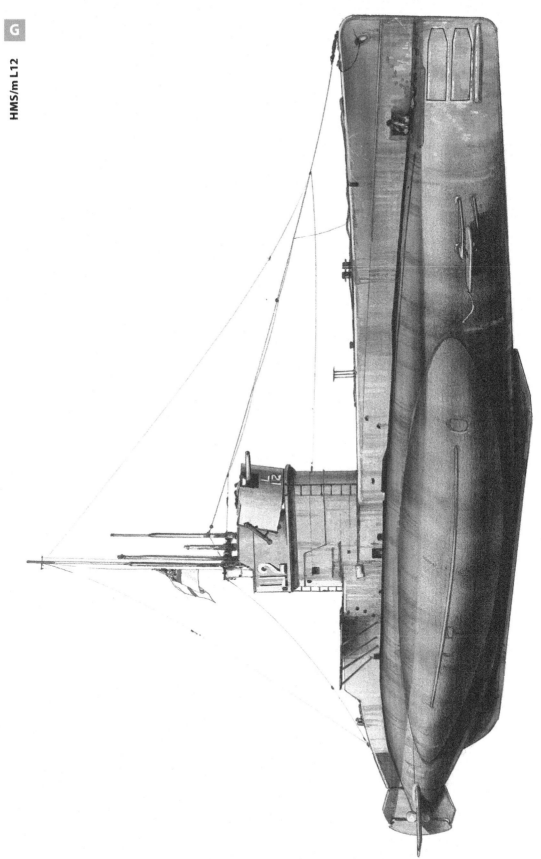

E20 06.11.15 Torpedoed by UB14 in the Sea of Marmora
E6   26.12.15 Mined in the North Sea
E17 06.01.16 Scuttled off Texel after running aground
E5   07.03.16 Mined in the North Sea
E24 24.03.16 Mined in the North Sea
E22 25.04.16 Torpedoed by UB18 in the North Sea
E18 24.05.16 Loss unknown – Baltic
E26 03.07.16 Loss unknown – North Sea
E16 22.08.16 Mined in the North Sea
E30 22.11.16 Loss unknown – North Sea
E37 01.12.16 Loss unknown – North Sea
E36 19.01.17 Collision in the North Sea with E43
E49 12.03.17 Mined off the Shetland Isles
E47 20.08.17 Loss unknown – North Sea
E14 28.01.18 Sunk by enemy gunfire in the Dardanelles
E50 31.01.18 Mined in the North Sea
E9   03.04.18 Scuttled in the Baltic
E19 03.04.18 Scuttled in the Baltic
E1   03.04.18 Scuttled in the Baltic
E8   04.04.18 Scuttled in the Baltic
E34 20.07.18 Mined in the North Sea

Fates of the H-Class submarines
H6   19.01.16 Run aground on Ameland Island
H3   15.07.16 Mined in the Adriatic
H10 19.01.18 Loss unknown – North Sea
H5   02.03.18 Sunk by collision in the Irish Sea

Fates of other classes
C31 04.01.15 Mined off Belgium
C33 04.08.15 Mined in the North Sea
C29 29.08.15 Mined in the North Sea
B10 09.08.16 Air raid on Venice
C34 17.07.17 Torpedoed by U52 off the Shetland Isles
G9   16.09.17 Sunk in error by HMS *Pasley* in the North Sea
C32 22.10.17 Scuttled off Riga
K1   18.11.17 Scuttled after collision with own forces in the North Sea
G8   14.01.18 Loss unknown – North Sea
K4   31.01.18 Collision off May Island
K17 31.01.18 Collision off May Island
C26 04.04.18 Scuttled in the Baltic
C27 05.04.18 Scuttled in the Baltic
C35 05.04.18 Scuttled in the Baltic
C3   23.04.18 Expended during Zeebrugge Raid
L10 03.10.18 Sunk by enemy action off the Dutch coast
J6   15.10.18 Sunk in error by the Q-ship HMS *Cymric* in the North Sea
G7   01.11.18 Loss unknown – North Sea

BIBLIOGRAPHY

Akermann, Paul, *Encyclopaedia of British Submarines 1901–1955*, Periscope Publishing, Cornwall (2002)

Ashmore, Vice Admiral L. H., *Forgotten Flotilla, British Submariners in Russia 1914–1919*, Royal Navy Submarine Museum (2001)

Blamey, Joel, *A Submariner's Story*, Periscope Publishing, Cornwall (2002)

Carr, W. G., *By Guess and by God*, Hutchinson, London (1930)

_____, *Hell's Angels of the Deep*, Hutchinson, London (1932)

Chalmers, RAdm W. S., *Max Horton and the Western Approaches*, Hodder & Stoughton, London (1954)

Cocker, M. P., *Royal Navy Submarines 1901–1982*, Warne, London (1982)

Compton-Hall, R., *Submarines at War 1914–1918*, Periscope Publishing, Cornwall (2004)

_____, *The First Submarines*, Periscope Publishing, Cornwall (2003)

Cowie, Capt J. S., *Mines, Minelayers and Minelaying*, OUP, Oxford (1949)

Davies, Roy, *Nautilus, The Story of Man Under the Sea*, BBC (1995)

Edwards, LtCdr K., *We Dive at Dawn*, Rich & Cowan, London (1939)

Evans, A. S., *Beneath the Waves, A History of HM Submarine Losses 1904–1971*, Periscope Publishing, Cornwall (2007)

Gibson, R. H. & Prendergast, M., *The German Submarine War 1914–1918*, Periscope Publishing, Cornwall (2002)

Gray, Edwyn, *Few Survived, A History of Submarine Disasters*, Leo Cooper, London (1986)

_____, *British Submarines in the Great War*, Pen & Sword, South Yorkshire (2001)

Grant, R. M., *U-Boats Destroyed*, Periscope Publishing, Cornwall (2002)

_____, *U-Boat Intelligence*, Periscope Publishing, Cornwall (2002)

_____, *U-Boat Hunters*, Periscope Publishing, Cornwall (2003)

Jameson, RAdm Sir William, *Submariners VC*, Periscope Publishing, Cornwall (2004)

_____, *The Dawn of the Submarine 1900–1918*, Periscope Publishing, Cornwall (2007)

Jane's Fighting Ships of World War One, Studio Editions, London (1993)

Kemp, LtCdr P. K., *H.M. Submarines*, Herbert Jenkins, London (1952)

Lambert, Dr N., *The Submarine Service 1900–1918*, Naval Records Society, Hampshire (2001)

Lipscomb, Cdr F. W., *The British Submarine*, A & C Black, London (1954)

Mackay, R., *A Precarious Existence, British Submariners in World War One*, Periscope Publishing, Cornwall (2003)

McCartney, Innes, *Lost Patrols, Submarine Wrecks of the English Channel*, Periscope Publishing, Cornwall (2003)

Smith, G., *Britain's Clandestine Submarines, 1914–1915*, Yale University Press, London (1964)

Young, Edward, *One of Our Submarines*, Rupert Hart-Davis, London (1962)

INDEX

References to illustrations are shown in **bold**.